Hello, Universe

Over 75
Quick Exercises
**to Manifest
Your Dreams**

Hello, Universe

Melanie Baker

CASTLE POINT BOOKS
NEW YORK

Hello, Universe

Copyright © 2022 by St. Martin's Press.
All rights reserved. Printed in Canada.
For information, address St. Martin's Publishing Group, 120 Broadway, New York, NY 10271.

www.castlepointbooks.com

The Castle Point Books trademark is owned by Castle Point Publishing, LLC.
Castle Point books are published and distributed by St. Martin's Publishing Group.

ISBN 978-1-250-28170-8 (trade paperback)

Design by Tara Long
Images used under license by Shutterstock.com

Our books may be purchased in bulk for promotional, educational, or business use. Please contact your local bookseller or the Macmillan Corporate and Premium Sales Department at 1-800-221-7945, extension 5442, or by email at MacmillanSpecialMarkets@macmillan.com.

First Edition: 2022

10 9 8 7 6 5 4 3 2 1

This journal belongs to:

....

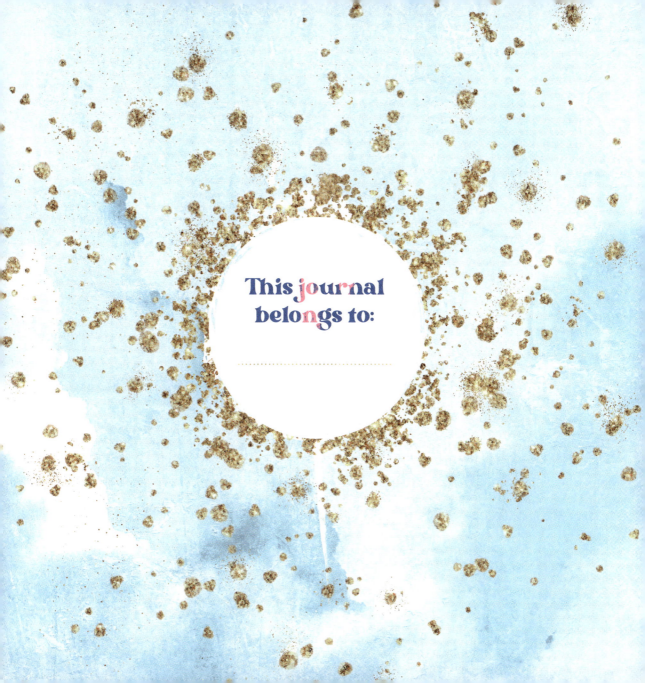

> When you want something, all the universe conspires in helping you to achieve it.

—PAULO COELHO

Introduction

THE UNIVERSE HAS BEEN WAITING FOR YOU! With its limitless magic, it can help you find the perfect job, manifest a windfall, visualize your way to great health, and live the life you have always imagined for yourself. You just have to start the conversation. And that's all manifestation is—a conversation with an old friend who wants for you what you want for yourself. No matter where you're starting from, you can create a life you love because you're not doing it alone.

With practical guidance, simple prompts, and inspiring quotes, *Hello, Universe* gives you the tools you need to speak the Universe's language, break down your limiting beliefs, and leverage the power you've held all along. Whether you work through these pages one by one or go where your intuition leads you, you'll find your mindset shifting toward clarity, abundance, and effortless manifestation. So, say hello to limitless possibilities and take control of your destiny!

It's already yours.

—THE UNIVERSE

Believe You Can

The first step in any manifesting journey is to start believing that you can have the things you want. Look back over your life and notice all the things—big and small—that made it from your wish list to reality. They could be anything, from a pair of really great jeans to a job you love. Write them down here as proof of previous manifestations.

Lift Yourself Up

The Universe won't hold a bad mood against you, but you manifest more easily and accurately when you're feeling good. Fill this page with things that can lift you up when you're feeling down, then refer back to it when you need a boost.

Go for a walk

> **Every single second is an opportunity to change your life, because in any moment you can change the way you feel.**
>
> —RHONDA BYRNE

> Thoughts become things.
> —MIKE DOOLEY

Reframe Negative Thoughts

Good or bad, your thoughts shape your reality. Be mindful of your inner narrative so your reality is shaped by your joy rather than your fear. What worries have been running through your head? How can you reframe them in a positive light?

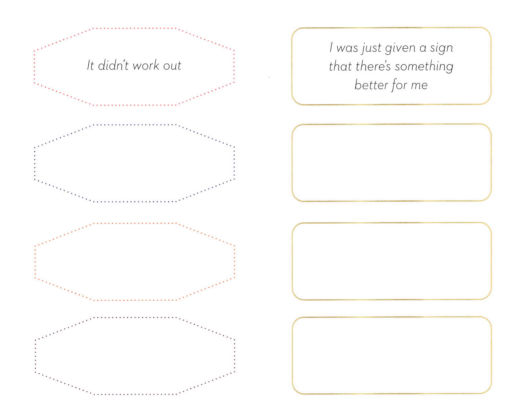

It didn't work out

I was just given a sign that there's something better for me

Name Your Limiting Beliefs

To break through limiting beliefs, you first have to identify them. What unhelpful attitudes are you holding on to? Being completely honest with yourself about your feelings, take a few minutes to complete the following statements.

MONEY IS ....

WORK IS ....

LIFE IS ....

LOVE IS ....

FAMILY IS ....

Notice any limiting beliefs?

....

....

....

....

> Whether you believe you can do a thing or not, you are right.
>
> —HENRY FORD

> **Not only are we in the Universe, the Universe is in us.**
>
> —NEIL DEGRASSE TYSON

Step into Your Power

Like the stars, the trees, and the oceans, human beings are made from the same stuff (matter) as the Universe itself. That means that the magic of the Universe courses through your veins and connects you to the world around you. Close your eyes and visualize that energetic current running through you. How does it make you feel?

Let Yourself Dream

When you choose to work with the Universe, no dream is too big. Fill this page with your wildest dreams. When you feel the pull to be more realistic or tempered, notice it and push through it. You'll train your mind to see possibilities instead of limitations.

> If you can dream it, you can do it.
>
> —SHERALYN SILVERSTEIN

“

Luck is the residue of design.

—JOHN MILTON

”

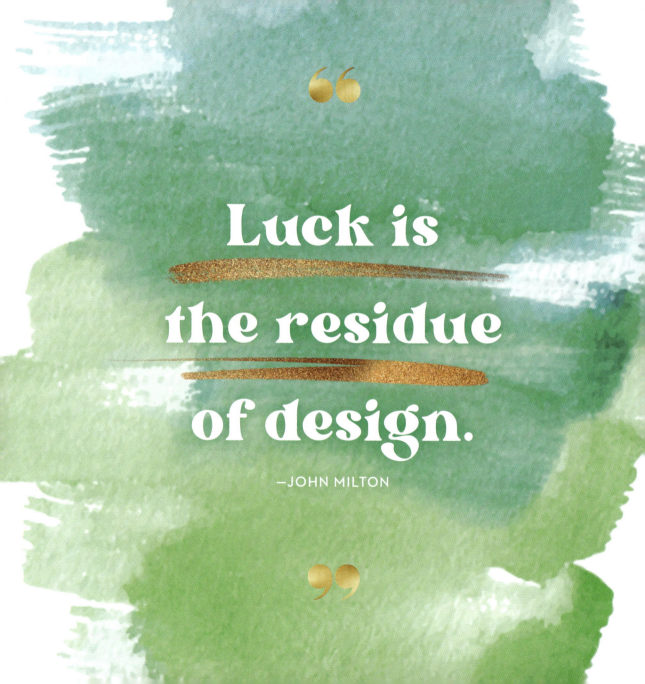

Spot the Synchronicities

Those little moments when you think, "Well, that was lucky"? Those are by design. From finding a great parking spot on a busy day to catching the exact movie you were just thinking of on TV, synchronicity is the Universe letting you know it's listening. Write down five synchronistic moments that prove the Universe has your back.

1. ....

2. ....

3. ....

4. ....

5. ....

Turn Thoughts into Intentions

Your biggest dreams may feel impossible, but everything that exists in the world began with a simple thought. Make a habit of turning wishful thinking into intention setting. Complete this sentence:

WOULDN'T IT BE NICE IF ....

....

....

Now turn your thought into an intention by framing it as if it's certain to happen. For example, "Wouldn't it be nice if I could afford to buy a house instead of renting?" becomes "I will own a house with a big backyard and covered porch."
The more specific you can get, the better!

I WILL ....

....

....

> You create your thoughts, your thoughts create your intentions, and your intentions create your reality.

—DR. WAYNE DYER

> **Get out of your head and get into your heart. Think less, feel more.**
>
> —OSHO

Get Emotional

Intentions are most effective when they're charged with emotion. Your head may be full of limiting beliefs, social conditioning, and rationalizations that make hard work of manifesting, but your heart knows your true desires. Write down three things you hope to manifest, focusing on how they make you feel.

1

2

3

Raise Your Vibration

When you raise your vibration (positive energy), the Universe will meet it. Want more love, happiness, and abundance in your life? Write down a few things that bring you joy now (bear hugs, really great coffee, etc.) and commit to experiencing them more often.

“

Do anything, but let it produce joy.

—HENRY MILLER

”

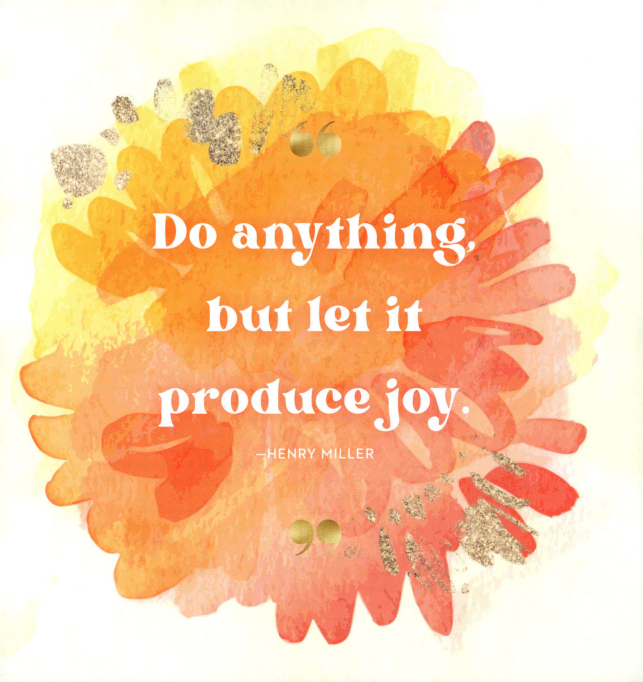

> **Everything amazing about the universe is inside of you, and the two are inseparable.**
>
> —CARL SAGAN

Know Your Worth

One of the biggest blocks people face is feeling unworthy of their dreams. But you are amazing, and you deserve to have your dreams come true. Rewrite the following affirmations word for word.

I AM LOVED AND SUPPORTED.

....

I AM POWERFUL.

....

I AM MORE THAN ENOUGH.

....

I AM WORTHY OF MY DREAMS.

....

Say these affirmations out loud to yourself at least once a day and as often as you need to hear them.

Challenge Your Beliefs

Human beings are hardwired to unconsciously look for proof of what we believe to be true. What are some things you'd *like* to believe? Write them here and then expect the Universe to give you proof to back them up.

....

....

....

....

....

....

....

....

....

"Expect good things."

—THE UNIVERSE

> **Ask for what you want and be prepared to get it.**
>
> —MAYA ANGELOU

Act as If

Acting as if you've already manifested something is one of the quickest ways to bring it into your life. What are five things you would be grateful to have or have happen in your life? Write them down as if they've already manifested, then visualize yourself enjoying each one.

1.
2.
3.
4.
5.

Be Kind to Yourself

While we easily shower friends with kind words and encouragement, we're often too hard on ourselves. So today, talk to yourself like you would a friend. Write down what you need to hear most.

_____

_____

_____

_____

_____

_____

_____

_____

_____

Practice speaking to yourself like a friend often. The Universe is listening!

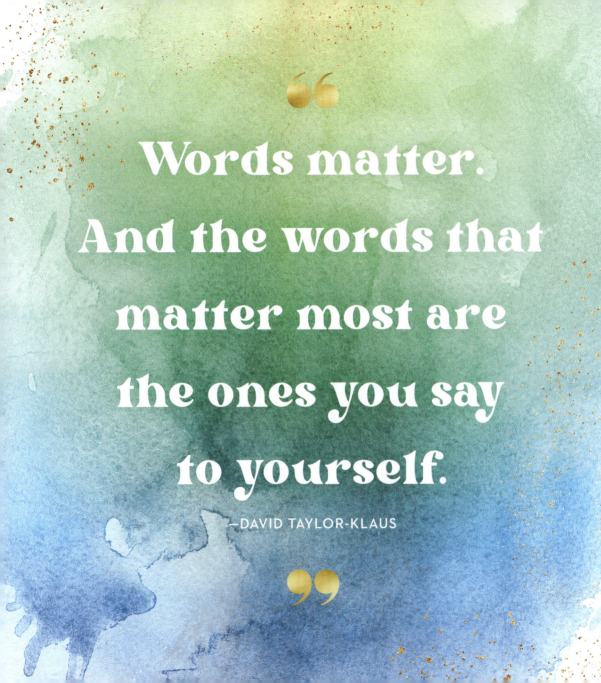

> Words matter. And the words that matter most are the ones you say to yourself.
>
> —DAVID TAYLOR-KLAUS

> Everything you'll ever need to know is within you; the secrets of the universe are imprinted on the cells of your body.
>
> —DAN MILLMAN

Learn to Trust Your Gut

Manifesting your greatest desires requires that you get clear on what those desires are. One way to do that is to learn how to listen to your gut (a.k.a. your intuition). Write about a time when you followed your intuition and were happy with the outcome.

....

....

....

....

....

....

....

....

Try to recognize that sense of intuition in the future.

Train Your Mind for Positivity

List ten things, big or small, that you're grateful for every day. Whenever you catch yourself focusing on what you don't have, come back to this list. Spend a few seconds concentrating on each item and why you're grateful for it.

> Be thankful for what you have; you'll end up having more. If you concentrate on what you don't have, you will never, ever have enough.

—OPRAH WINFREY

> Go confidently in the direction of your dreams. Live the life you have imagined.
>
> —HENRY DAVID THOREAU

Have Confidence in Your Dreams

Our dreams are our own, but we often internalize the desires of others. In one column, write down what you think other people want for you. In the other column, write down what you (and only you) want. Starting today, go confidently in the direction of *your* dreams.

Write Your Story

The things you manifest are often based on the stories you tell yourself. What is your story right now? How does it make you feel?

Write a New Story

It's time to write a new story—the story of your life as you truly want it to be. Make sure you use the present tense ("I am" instead of "I will") and as much detail as possible.

Start Co-Creating Your Life

You're not in this alone. The Universe is conspiring to give you everything you want, making connections you can't even fathom. So let go of the logistics. What would you try to manifest if you didn't have to worry about how to make it happen? (Because you don't.)

> Learn how to see. Realize that everything connects to everything else.

—LEONARDO DA VINCI

> The fastest way to get to a new-and-improved situation is to make peace with your current situation.

—ESTHER HICKS

Keep Moving Forward

You can't manifest better things if you're hung up on what didn't work out in the past. Write down all the things you feel are keeping you from moving forward.

....

....

....

....

....

....

....

....

Resolve to leave the past here on this page and focus on building the future you want.

Embrace the New You

Growth can be uncomfortable, especially if it means growing apart from loved ones. But allowing yourself to bloom gives them permission to do the same. What traits and habits do you hope to cultivate in You 2.0?

> "You will evolve past certain people. Let yourself."
>
> —MANDY HALE

> Most people are thinking about what they don't want, and they're wondering why it shows up over and over again.
>
> —JOHN ASSARAF

Get Curious about Complaints

Venting is not only healthy, but it's also helpful. Look at your complaints from a different perspective: knowing what you *don't* want can help you figure out what you *do* want. Use this page to transform your irritations into intentions.

I hate being micromanaged. ➡ *My next manager will trust my work.*

Celebrate the Little Wins

When gratitude feels like too much to ask, practice turning your attention to the little things. Maybe there was no line at the grocery store, or you finished a project earlier than expected. Write down five recent wins, taking a moment to feel grateful for each.

1. ....

2. ....

3. ....

4. ....

5. ....

"Through the eyes of gratitude, everything is a miracle."

—MARY DAVIS

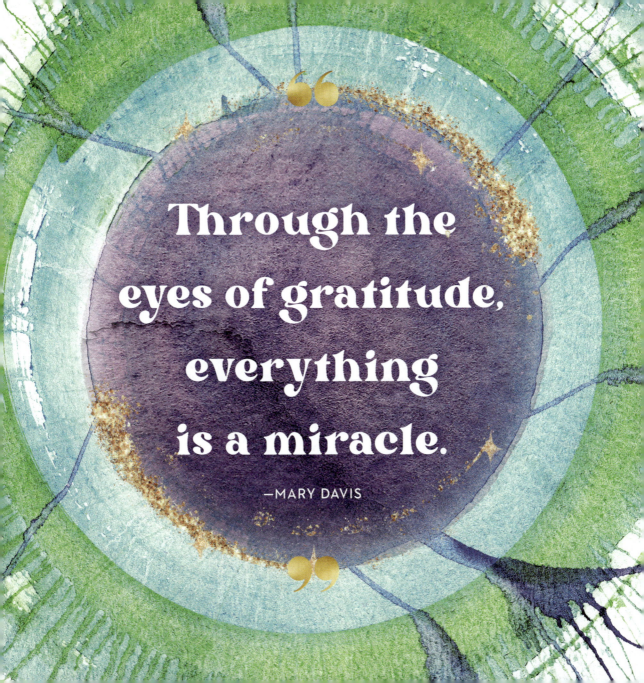

> If you could see the potential within you, it would amaze you to see all that you are capable of being.
>
> —CATHERINE PULSIFER

See the Future

Close your eyes and picture your ideal future. You've manifested your greatest dreams, have reached your full potential, and are blissfully happy. Describe what you saw in as much detail as possible. Return to this exercise often, tweaking your description as your dreams evolve.

Take Aligned Action

Once you ask for help in manifesting something, you need to meet the Universe halfway. What are some small steps you can take right now to show the Universe you mean business?

INTENTION	ACTION
Travel to Europe	*Renew my passport*

"

Get ready.

—THE UNIVERSE

"

> The universe buries strange jewels deep within us all, and then stands back to see if we can find them.
>
> —ELIZABETH GILBERT

Dig Deep

Figuring out what you really want can be more difficult than manifesting it. When you decide that you want something, ask yourself why. If you can trace the reason back to another person's expectations or your own limiting beliefs, keep digging.

I WANT

BECAUSE

I WANT

BECAUSE

I WANT

BECAUSE

I WANT

BECAUSE

Trust the Process

While we're busy playing checkers, the Universe is playing chess. And it's always making moves for your higher good, even when it doesn't feel like it. List at least three times not getting what you wanted was a blessing in disguise.

....

....

....

....

....

....

....

Whenever things don't work out in the future, rest assured that they'll make this list someday.

> The Universe's timing is perfect, even if it doesn't suit your ego.
>
> —DEAN JACKSON

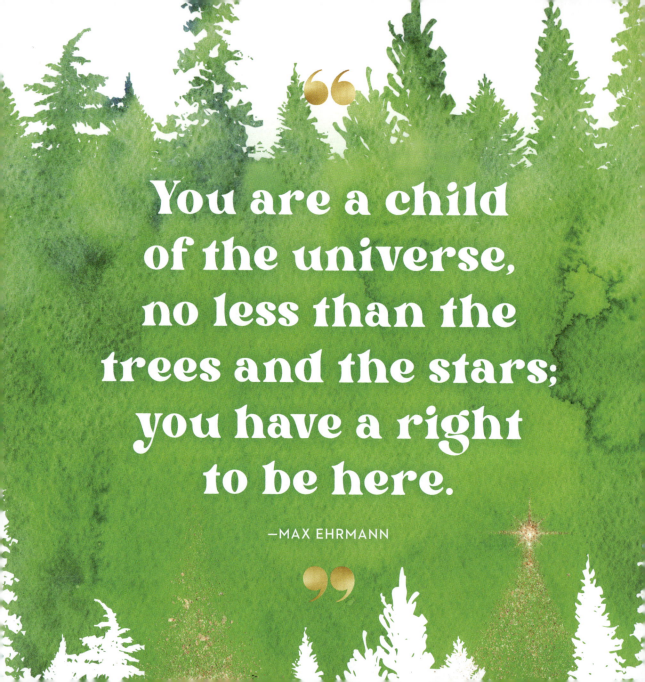

> You are a child of the universe, no less than the trees and the stars; you have a right to be here.

—MAX EHRMANN

Turn Blocks into Mantras

As a child of the Universe, you also have the right to ask for its help. Whenever you bump into self-doubt, try to understand what you're feeling. Then come up with a mantra to combat that feeling.

FEELING	MANTRA
Powerless	*I am powerful*

Repeat your mantras out loud daily until you feel a shift in your beliefs.

Focus on Your Why

When you focus on the feeling of being happy and let go of what that looks like, you manifest happiness in ways you can't even imagine. Start now. Fill this space with things that brighten your day, then either do them or visualize yourself doing them.

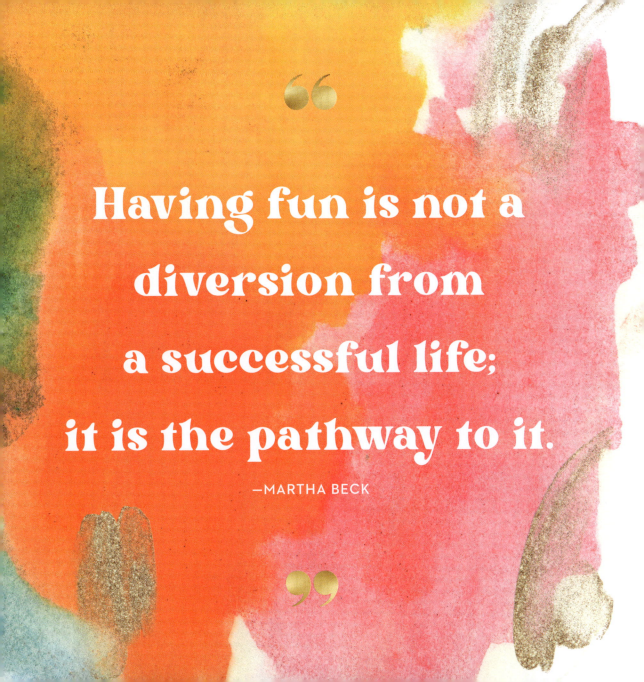

> Having fun is not a diversion from a successful life; it is the pathway to it.
>
> —MARTHA BECK

> To a mind that is still, the whole universe surrenders.

—CHUANG TZU

Listen Quietly

Meditation quiets the mind so that you can hear the Universe when it speaks to you. (It tends to speak softly.) You don't need to devote an hour each day to your practice. Start with five minutes of quiet time, and just listen. Write down whatever thoughts and feelings come up.

See Life without Limits

Once you've identified your limiting beliefs, write them down here. Then cross them out and write limitless beliefs next to them.

Money will always be tight. ➡ *I will always have more than enough money.*

➡

➡

➡

➡

➡

Repeat the new beliefs to yourself often to create new pathways in your brain.

“You manifest what you believe, not what you want.”

—SONIA RICOTTI

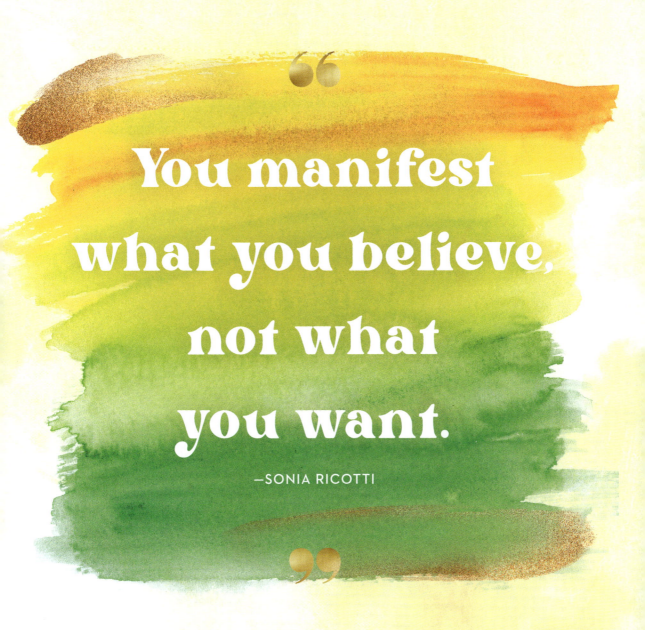

> To accomplish great things we must not only act, but also dream; not only plan, but also believe.
>
> —ANATOLE FRANCE

Use Your Imagination

As we get older, we often lose the childlike wonder that allows our imagination (and therefore, our visualization skills) to flourish. Think of something you'd like to manifest and tap into that childhood habit of letting your mind wander as far as it wants to go. Write down what you imagined.

Change "I Want" to "I Will"

How you frame your intentions lets the Universe know how serious you are about getting what you want. Starting with the words "I want," write about something you hope to manifest.

I WANT ....

....

I WANT ....

....

Write the same intention again, but this time, begin with "I will" or "I am."

....

....

....

....

Read both out loud. Do you feel the difference?

"Our intention is everything. Nothing happens on this planet without it."

—JIM CARREY

> "If we would just take a moment to look around, we would find that the universe is in constant communication with us."
>
> —ALEXANDRIA HOTMER

Recognize the Universe's Voice

The Universe speaks to us in all kinds of ways—signs, opportunities, synchronicities. It'll be easier to recognize these in the future if you notice how they've shown up in the past. Can you think of three times in your life you feel the Universe was trying to get your attention?

Hand Off the Hard Stuff

At a certain point in every manifestation, you have to let go and let the Universe do its part. Are you holding on too tightly to the outcome you want? Name three things you have no control over, and resolve to let the Universe handle them from here.

1

2

3

"

Let go.

—THE UNIVERSE

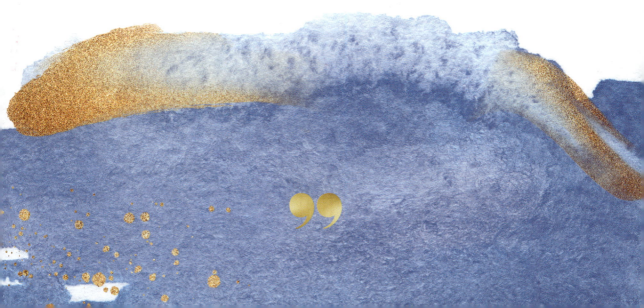

"

“

**Start where you are.
Use what you have.
Do what you can.**

—ARTHUR ASHE

”

Focus on the Present

You can't control when or how your intentions will manifest, so focus on what you can control—your actions in this moment. What can you do right now to bring your manifestation to life, even in the smallest way? For example, if you want to manifest a relaxing vacation, you could treat yourself to a massage or a candlelit bath.

Level Up Your Self-Care

Are you ready to receive all the Universe has to offer? Getting into better shape physically, mentally, and spiritually can help you level up your manifestation practice. Create a short-term goal for each of the following categories.

PHYSICAL HEALTH

....

....

....

MENTAL HEALTH

....

....

....

SPIRITUAL HEALTH

....

....

....

Make It a Habit

Now create a long-term goal for each category.

PHYSICAL HEALTH

....

....

....

MENTAL HEALTH

....

....

....

SPIRITUAL HEALTH

....

....

....

Spend at least a few minutes each day working toward your goals and watch your manifestation powers grow!

> Patience is not waiting. Patience is active acceptance of the process required to attain your goals and dreams.
>
> —RAY DAVIS

Stay Motivated

Manifestation isn't often quick work. The Universe is tirelessly manipulating the Rubik's Cube of your life to get you what you want. All it asks in return is that you keep the faith. Visualize your intention finally manifesting again now. What makes it worth the wait?

Choose Constructive Thoughts

The good news is, positive thoughts can snowball just as easily as negative ones. But while negative thoughts are destructive (think: avalanche), positive thoughts are constructive (think: snowman). When you start to feel negativity snowballing, come to this page and write down three positive thoughts, letting them build on each other.

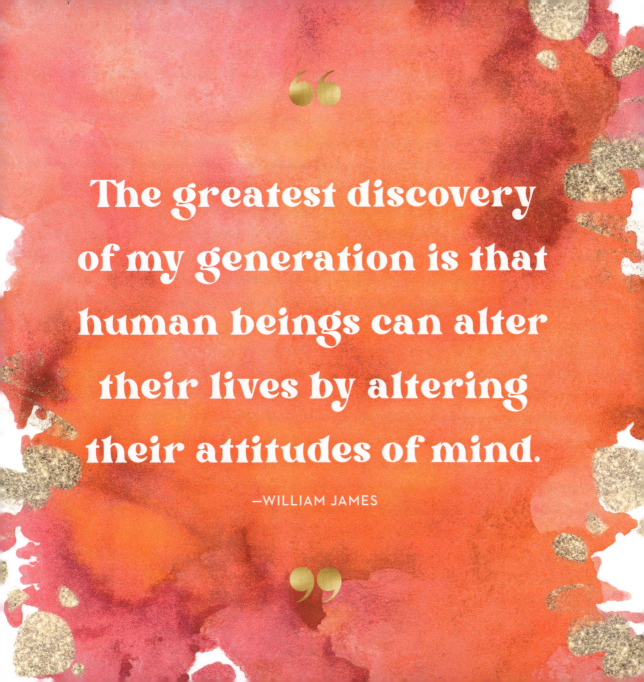

> The greatest discovery of my generation is that human beings can alter their lives by altering their attitudes of mind.
>
> —WILLIAM JAMES

> Do not feel lonely, the entire universe is inside of you.
>
> —RUMI

Be What You Need

One of the quickest ways to manifest love, happiness, friendship, or kindness is to give those things to others. After all, you are an extension of the Universe and have access to its magic. What feeling are you hoping to manifest?

....

....

....

List three ways you can help others feel that way.

1 ....

2 ....

3 ....

Craft Your Masterpiece

Visualization is just the practice of seeing a clear and detailed picture in your mind of what you want to manifest. Refine your intention like Michelangelo creating a work of art—hold it in your mind and chip away at anything that doesn't get you closer to it. What does your masterpiece look like?

> "Everyone visualizes whether he knows it or not. Visualizing is the great secret of success."
>
> —Geneviève Behrend

> Imagination is everything. It is the preview of life's coming attractions.
>
> —ALBERT EINSTEIN

Make Time to Daydream

Daydreaming may be problematic in a classroom, but it's a powerful tool in your manifestation practice. So let yourself do it more often. It's the first step in visualizing your desired outcome.

What do you tend to daydream about?

If it enters your mind, it's there for a reason. What is your daydream telling you?

Walk in Faith

The Universe has already set things in motion so that what you are seeking is seeking you. Now you have to take the first few real steps in its direction, even if it's a little intimidating. What is a slightly bigger step you can take on faith toward your manifestation?

> Take the first step in faith. You don't have to see the whole staircase. Just take the first step.

—DR. MARTIN LUTHER KING JR.

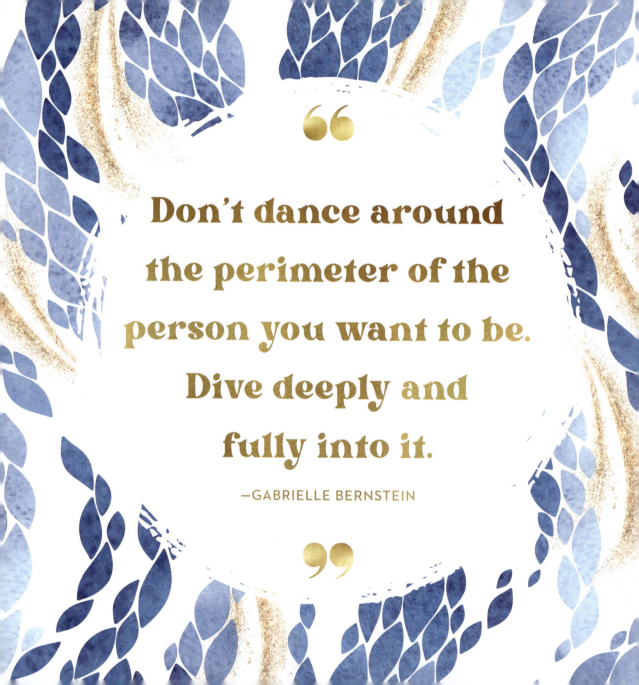

> Don't dance around the perimeter of the person you want to be. Dive deeply and fully into it.
>
> —GABRIELLE BERNSTEIN

Step into Your Future Self

Take a moment to visualize in detail who you hope to become once you've manifested your greatest dreams. How is Future You different from Current You?

....

....

....

....

....

....

....

....

Try to incorporate some of the traits of Future You into your daily life now. When you speak, act, or think, channel the version of yourself you truly want to be.

Have Some Perspective

Worrying about something only gives it power and makes you more likely to manifest reasons to worry. When you feel yourself worrying, take three slow, deep breaths and then take the long view of the issue.

WHAT ARE YOU WORRIED ABOUT TODAY?

....

....

....

WILL IT MATTER A YEAR FROM NOW?

....

....

....

FIVE YEARS FROM NOW?

....

....

....

> **If you want to test your memory, try to recall what you were worrying about one year ago today.**
>
> —E. JOSEPH COSSMAN

> To bring something into your life, imagine that it's already there.
>
> —RICHARD BACH

Fake It 'Til You Make It

When it feels impossible to act as if you already have what you're working so hard to manifest, focus on the ripple effects of your manifestation. What benefits will manifesting your intention have? How can you experience some of those benefits now?

Say "Yes" to the Universe

You never know when the Universe will present you with the next step in your manifestation journey, so you need to stay open to the possibility. What have you said "yes" to in the past that has turned out to be a wonderful opportunity?

....

....

....

....

....

....

....

....

....

....

Practice saying "yes" to new opportunities whenever you can.

> A key to manifestation is that when the doors of opportunity open, you have to walk through them.
>
> —RUSSELL ERIC DOBDA

> **If it's out of your hands, it deserves freedom from your mind too.**
>
> —IVAN NURU

Leave Room for Magic

When you let the Universe surprise you, what it gives you could exceed your wildest dreams. List three things you can focus on (like setting new intentions or visualizing outcomes) instead of micromanaging your manifestations.

1.

2.

3.

Focus on Your Feelings

Even when you're not clear on what you want to happen, you know instinctively how you want to feel. Focus on that and let the Universe work out the details. Which of the feelings below resonates with you? Circle them and set an intention to feel that way.

HAPPY

JOYFUL

EXCITED

ENTHUSIASTIC

CALM

RELAXED

BALANCED

LOVED

SUPPORTED

FULFILLED

“

You feel before you think.

—DANIELLE LAPORTE

”

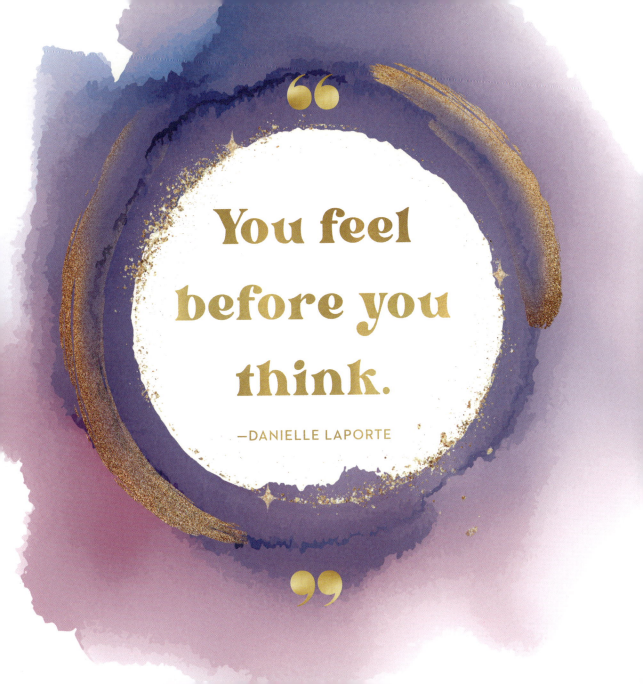

> It is the combination of thought and love which forms the irresistible force of the law of attraction.

—CHARLES HAMMEL

Treat Yourself Well

Manifestation is a labor of love. You are loved by the Universe, and that love courses through you and everything you do. Treating yourself well shows the Universe that you know you're worthy of it. What are some ways you can take care of yourself?

✦ *Take a yoga class*

✦ *Splurge on the latte*

✦

✦

✦

✦

✦

✦

✦

✦

Do the Work

You can't "set it and forget it" when it comes to your intention. Manifesting the life you want is the active practice of co-creating it with the Universe. How can you show up for your intention today?

"

I'll meet you there.

—THE UNIVERSE

"

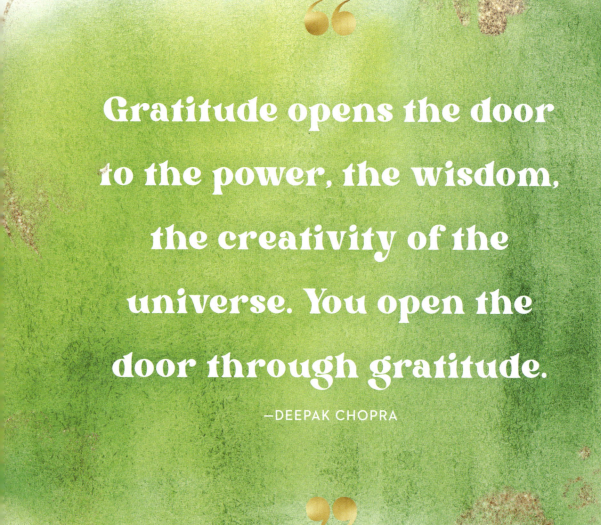

> Gratitude opens the door to the power, the wisdom, the creativity of the universe. You open the door through gratitude.
>
> —DEEPAK CHOPRA

Get into a Gratitude Flow

Gratitude itself does a lot of the legwork for you; its energy opens you up to receive more gifts from the Universe. Answer the following questions to get that gratitude flowing.

WHAT ARE YOU THANKFUL FOR IN THIS MOMENT?

WHAT IS GOING WELL IN YOUR LIFE?

WHAT ARE YOU EXCITED ABOUT?

HOW CAN YOU CELEBRATE IT?

Embrace Whatever Comes

When a manifestation is close to realization, you may notice things around you going haywire. Some things have to break down to make room for your dreams. Your job is to persevere and prepare for them. Write a mantra here that will get you through those tough times.

> It's not what happens to you, but how you react to it that matters.
>
> —EPICTETUS

“The future depends on what you do today.”

—MAHATMA GANDHI

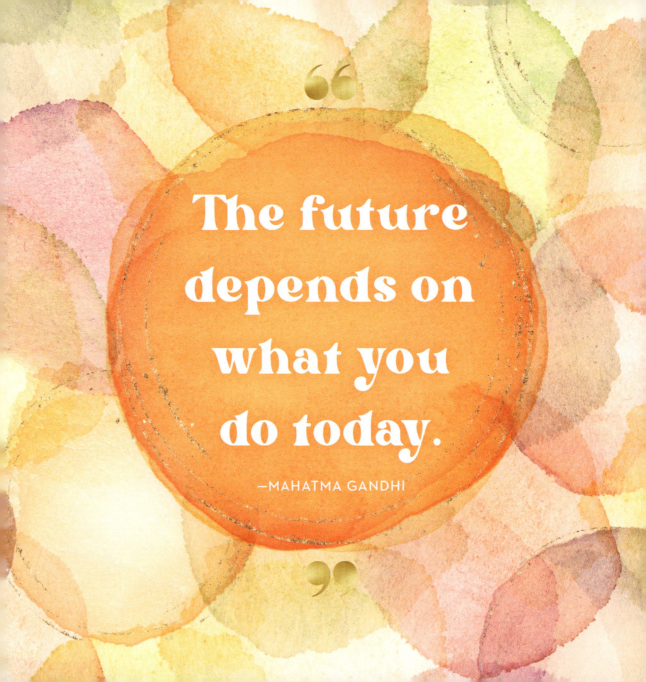

Make Every Day Count

Every day is a fresh start, a new opportunity to manifest the things you want most in life. What will you do with your fresh start today? Use this space to brainstorm.

Make a Blueprint

You've probably heard of vision boards (collages of photos and words that represent what you hope to manifest). These can be powerful tools for focusing your mind, especially once you've gotten clear on your intentions. Use the space below to make a list of the things you want to include or to sketch out how you want it to look.

Spend at least 15 minutes a day with your vision board, infusing each element on it with emotion as well as positive energy.

> Cherish your visions and your dreams as they are the children of your soul, the blueprints of your ultimate achievements.
>
> —NAPOLEON HILL

Make a New To-Do List

Instead of making a list of things you want to manifest, try making a list of things you want to experience. It can include feelings, flavors, places—you name it. Take a minute to visualize each experience and see which ones resonate with you most.

Create New Pathways

Take one of the experiences on your list and write a story about it in the space below, using as much detail as you can muster. Practice visualizing like this often to create new, more manifestation-friendly pathways in your brain.

> Your life is the manifestation of your dream; it is an art. You can change your life anytime that you're not enjoying the dream.
>
> —DON MIGUEL RUIZ

Find Flexibility

Whether you've made a manifestation mistake or you've simply evolved since you first set your intention, it is never too late to start again. Take what you've learned so far and set a new intention below.

Cultivate Healthy Friendships

Surrounding yourself with loving, supportive people helps you stay in the right frame of mind for manifesting.

WHO FITS THAT DESCRIPTION?

....

....

....

....

WHO DOESN'T?

....

....

....

....

Limit your time with anyone who leaves you feeling cynical or exhausted. If you look closely, they may also be the source of some of your limiting beliefs.

Let us be grateful to people who make us happy; they are the charming gardeners who make our souls blossom.

—MARCEL PROUST

> Throw your dreams into space like a kite, and you do not know what it will bring back— a new life, a new friend, a new love, a new country.
>
> —ANAÏS NIN

Welcome the Universe's Wisdom

Sometimes the Universe knows what you need better than you do. By now you know to focus on the why and leave the how alone. Now celebrate the ways in which the Universe has surprised you with something even more wonderful than you could ever have imagined.

Come back to this page whenever your faith in the process begins to falter.

Look with Fresh Eyes

The only limitations you face are the ones taking up residence in your own mind. Write down any doubts you have below, then challenge them with what you've learned so far.

> Stop waiting for somebody to elevate your game. You are already equipped with everything you need to manifest your own greatness.

—GERMANY KENT

> "The body says what words cannot.
>
> —MARTHA GRAHAM"

Get Out of Your Head

The Universe often whispers to us through our own intuition. Tune into yours by getting out of your head and into your body. Hold your intention or next move in your mind. Do you notice any changes in how you feel?

....

....

....

....

....

....

....

....

Feeling calm or expansive are good signs; feeling anxious or contracted are good indications that you need to dig deeper.

Grow Your Own Way

The things you choose to manifest have to come from your heart. If you find yourself feeling competitive in your practice, try to get to the root of it.

WHO ARE YOU TRYING TO COMPETE WITH?

WHY IS "WINNING" IMPORTANT TO YOU?

HOW WILL "WINNING" MAKE YOU FEEL?

CAN YOU FEEL THIS WAY WITHOUT COMPETING?

By understanding the feeling you're chasing, you can set an intention that's true to you.

> A flower does not think of competing with the flower next to it. It just blooms.
>
> —ZEN SHIN

> Whatever you can do, or dream you can, begin it. Boldness has genius, power, and magic in it. Begin it now.

—JOHANN WOLFGANG VON GOETHE

Start Today

Sometimes, the only thing standing in your way is you. What dreams have you put on hold because you don't feel ready to commit to them?

What can you do right now to set them in motion? Start before you're ready!

Choose Compassion Over Judgment

Negative self-talk can stop your manifestations in their tracks. Notice when you're judging your dreams rather than supporting them. Write down your inner critic's words, then counter them with compassion.

> We ask ourselves, Who am I to be brilliant, gorgeous, handsome, talented, and fabulous? Actually, who are you not to be?

—MARIANNE WILLIAMSON

> Happiness is your birthright.
> —THE UNIVERSE

Choose Your Own Adventure

The Universe wants you to be happy as much as you want to be happy. Visualize yourself having lived a long, healthy, happy life, then use the space below to write a mini biography. What are the highlights of your happy life?

Ask for Help

When you're having trouble hearing the Universe speaking to you (or through you), find a quiet place to sit for a few minutes, preferably outdoors with the sun on your face. Hold your question gently in your mind while you take five slow, deep breaths. Write down anything that comes to you in those moments.

> Quiet the mind, and the soul will speak.
>
> —MA JAYA SATI BHAGAVATI

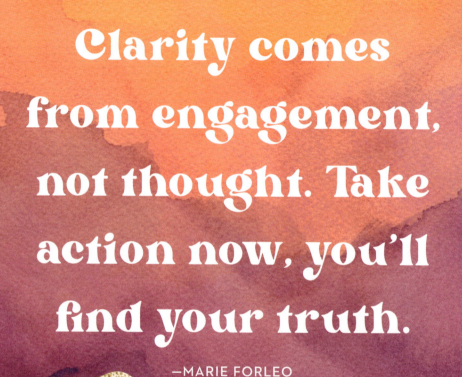

Clarity comes from engagement, not thought. Take action now, you'll find your truth.

—MARIE FORLEO

Try Something New

Meditation and introspection are wonderful tools for getting clear on what you want in life, but they're not the only ones. Sometimes the best way to find out whether something is for you is to try it. Once you have, answer these questions:

DID YOU ENJOY THE EXPERIENCE?

HOW DID IT MAKE YOU FEEL?

WHAT HAS IT TAUGHT YOU?

Notice Self-Defeating Patterns

Do you keep coming up against closed doors? The Universe may be guiding you to the one that's meant for you. But make sure you're not getting in your own way by checking in with your beliefs again. Complete the following statements without looking at your previous answers.

MONEY IS ....

WORK IS ....

LIFE IS ....

LOVE IS ....

FAMILY IS ....

Focus your efforts on combating any beliefs that haven't evolved with all your hard work.

> Just be honest with yourself. That opens the door.

—VERNON HOWARD

> The world is full of magical things patiently waiting for our wits to grow sharper.
>
> —EDEN PHILLPOTTS

Reconnect with the Magic

Wherever you are, take a few moments to be fully present. Tap into your senses one by one, appreciating what they discover. Then write down what you experienced. Repeat this exercise whenever you want to feel connected to the magic of the Universe.

WHAT DID YOU SEE? ....

....

WHAT DID YOU SMELL? ....

....

WHAT DID YOU HEAR? ....

....

WHAT DID YOU TASTE? ....

....

WHAT DID YOU FEEL? ....

....

Give Yourself Permission

You have the Universe's blessing to ask for whatever your heart desires. But sometimes, you need to give *yourself* permission to want what you want. Make a list of your wildest dreams and deepest wishes—including the ones you haven't told anyone. Then write "YES!" next to each one.

> **If you don't ask, the answer is always no.**
>
> —NORA ROBERTS

> There is nothing in a caterpillar that tells you it's going to be a butterfly.

—R. BUCKMINSTER FULLER

Surrender to the Greater Plan

Once you've done everything you can—you've set your intention, visualized the outcome, and taken aligned action—it's time to let the Universe take the wheel. Remind yourself of its awesome power by listing five of its most incredible creations.

1.

2.

3.

4.

5.

Avoid the Shoulds

Whenever you hear yourself saying or thinking "I should," strike that intention from your mind and your manifestations. It's a telltale sign of worrying about what others think instead of focusing on what you truly want. Write down all the things you feel you should do, then scribble them out and write down what you want to do.

> Don't let the noise of others' opinions drown out your own inner voice.
>
> —STEVE JOBS

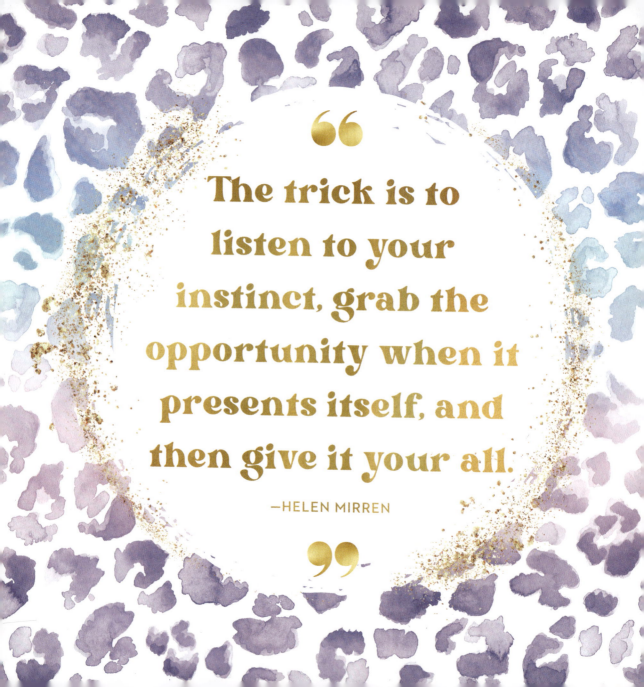

> The trick is to listen to your instinct, grab the opportunity when it presents itself, and then give it your all.
>
> —HELEN MIRREN

Go All In

The Universe knows we humans have our doubts and hesitations, which is why it offers us proof every day of the miracles we can create together. Now that you've seen it in action, it's time to go big. What's a dream you've been holding back?

....

....

....

....

SET AN INTENTION RIGHT NOW TO MANIFEST IT.

....

....

....

....

Take your first step toward that dream today!

Do It Scared

With the Universe by your side, you have no reason to be scared. But that doesn't mean you won't be. The trick is to push through the fear and continue moving in the direction of your dreams.

What is something you've been wanting to manifest but you're scared or worried about?

....

....

....

....

What is one step you can take today to move that manifestation forward?

....

....

....

....

> "Worry is like a rocking chair: it gives you something to do but never gets you anywhere."
>
> —ERMA BOMBECK

> All that we are is the result of what we have thought.
>
> —BUDDHA

Ask "What If?"

We ask ourselves "what if" all the time, but it's usually a way of talking ourselves out of doing what we want to do. For every negative "what if" you can come up with, counter it with a positive "what if."

WHAT IF IT DOESN'T WORK OUT?

WHAT IF IT WORKS OUT EVEN BETTER THAN I EXPECTED?

Continue the Conversation

You are never alone—not for a single minute of your life. The Universe is listening to you, loving you, and supporting you every step of the way. In your own words, write an affirmation to that effect so you can come back to it whenever you feel lost or alone on your journey.

“I’ve got this.”

—THE UNIVERSE

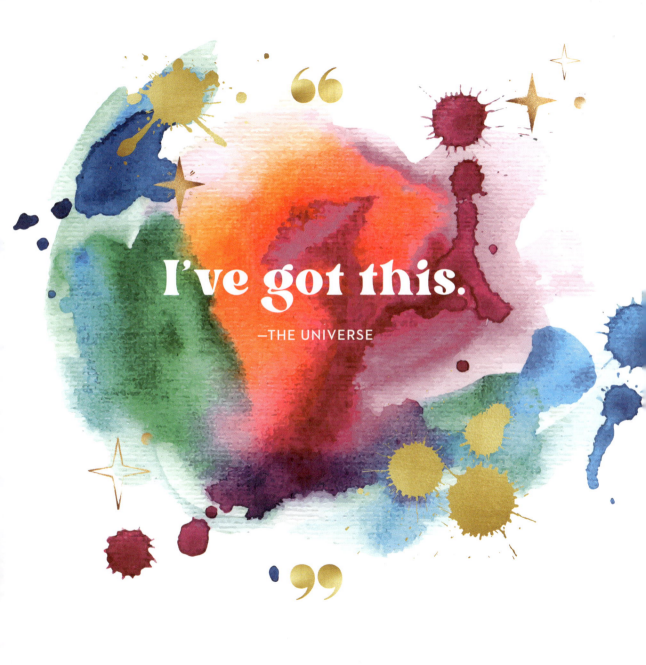

Keep Going

If you could give your younger self one lesson in manifesting, what would it be?

....

....

....

....

....

....

....

Both your dreams and your manifestation practice grow and evolve with you. Go back and complete these exercises again every so often. Fill these pages with proof of the Universe's love for you and of your own power. And continue to co-create the life you want every day!